THE INDUSTRIAL REVOLUTION

Volume 9

The Industrial Revolution and the Working Class

James R. Arnold & Roberta Wiener

Grolier

An imprint of Scholastic Library Publishing
Danbury, Connecticut

First published in 2005 by Grolier
An imprint of Scholastic Library Publishing
Old Sherman Turnpike
Danbury, Connecticut 06816

For information address the publisher:
Scholastic Library Publishing, Old Sherman Turnpike,
Danbury, Connecticut 06816

Library of Congress Cataloging-in-Publication Data

Arnold, James R.
    The industrial revolution / James R. Arnold and Roberta Wiener.
      p. cm
    Includes bibliographical references and index.
    Contents: v. 1. A turning point in history – v. 2. The industrial revolution begins – v. 3. The industrial revolution spreads – v. 4. The industrial revolution comes to America – v. 5. The growth of the industrial revolution in America – v. 6. The industrial revolution spreads through Europe – v. 7. The worldwide industrial revolution – v. 8. America's second industrial revolution – v. 9. The industrial revolution and the working class v. 10. The industrial revolution and American society.
    ISBN 0-7172-6031-3 (set)—ISBN 0-7172-6032-1 (v. 1)—
ISBN 0-7172-6033-X (v. 2)—ISBN 0-7172-6034-8 (v. 3)—
ISBN 0-7172-6035-6 (v. 4)—ISBN 0-7172-6036-4 (v. 5)—
ISBN 0-7172-6037-2 (v. 6)—ISBN 0-7172-6038-0 (v. 7)—
ISBN 0-7172-6039-9 (v. 8)—ISBN 0-7172-6040-2 (v. 9)—
ISBN 0-7172-6041-0 (v. 10)
    1. Industrial revolution. 2. Economic history. I. Wiener, Roberta.
II. Title.

HD2321.A73 2005
330.9'034–dc22   2004054243

Printed and bound in China

CONTENTS

THE SATANIC MILLS AND THE CRYSTAL PALACE

The British Industrial Revolution was in full flight over the years 1804 to 1808 when the poet William Blake composed the following stanzas:

And did those feet in ancient time
Walk upon England's mountains green?
And was the holy Lamb of God
On England's pleasant pastures seen?

And did the coutenenance divine
Shine forth upon our clouded hills?
And was Jerusalem builded here
Among those dark Satanic mills?

The Industrial Revolution was one of the rare times in world history when the human species changed the boundaries of its existence. Alongside the revolution in technology was a revolution in the organization of production. The factory

Below left: Manchester's population grew dramatically during the Industrial Revolution as people flocked to the city to work in the cotton mills. In 1835 a writer described Manchester's working-class neighborhood: "The population is crowded into one dense mass, in cottages separated by narrow, unpaved, and almost pestilential streets; in an atmosphere loaded with the smoke and exhalations of a large manufacturing city."

symbolized the Industrial Revolution. There large groups of workers labored in new ways, subject to factory discipline and unprecedented specialization of labor in order to work faster and in a more coordinated way. The Industrial Revolution most dramatically changed the lives of the working class. They were the ones who labored in the "dark Satanic mills." Workers reacted to the changes with a full range of behavior from simple violence to constructive organization.

THE GREAT EXHIBITION

In Great Britain 1850 marked the completion of a well-defined phase of economic development. The use of steam power and specialized machinery was common. Capitalists understood the techniques of large-scale manufacture so well that Great

Below: At the time of the Great Exhibition of 1851 a London newspaper described the British empire as "the mightiest empire of the globe—the empire in which industry is the most successfully cultivated, and in which its triumphs have been greatest." By 1851 British industry produced about half of all manufactured goods traded worldwide. Inside the Crystal Palace.

Britain accounted for about one-third of the world's industrial production. So Great Britain proudly demonstrated its position as "the workshop of the world" by holding a technological show that became known as the Great Exhibition. Six million visitors walked through a giant glass structure more than a third of a mile long and 66 feet high called the "Crystal Palace" in London's Hyde Park. More than half of the 14,000 exhibitors were either British or British colonists.

The Crystal Palace, filled with technological marvels, was itself a marvel.

Indeed, in this year Great Britain was the richest nation on earth in terms of income per person, the fastest growing in terms of the percentage of national product generated by industry, and the most urbanized. Its population had nearly tripled since 1780, the average income more than doubled. Great Britain mined about two-thirds of the world's coal and produced half of its iron and cotton cloth.

Middle- and upper-class England were proud of the Great Exhibition. The prosperity of the Industrial Revolution had propelled between one in five and one in six people into the middle class, a higher percentage than ever before. The middle and upper classes generally believed that the marvelous science and technology on display were proof that the world was improving rapidly. Outside of the Crystal Palace they saw increasing quantities and varieties of material goods, many of which made their lives easier and more enjoyable. The Great Exhibition was a symbol of welcome progress, and they rapidly pushed on with the task of enlarging industry and trade.

Capitalism was the basis of industry and trade. Profit came from efficiency, and factory discipline relentlessly promoted this efficiency. Many religious leaders likewise supported factory discipline because it accorded with the prevailing Evangelical view that "a soul reborn to God," as they put it, had to forsake immoderate habits. In place of such behaviors as drunkenness and sloth factory discipline taught desirable routines including hard work, self-discipline, and thriftiness.

In addition, the middle class was adopting the values of discipline in the belief that a sober way of life benefited all classes. They could point to the man who had designed the Crystal Palace itself, Joseph Paxton, as a living example of how someone could rise from humble origins. Paxton had begun his working life as a lowly gardener, taught himself biology and engineering, and combined that knowledge with a shrewd sense of business to make the Crystal Palace a British symbol of industrial prosperity.

Eight years later a Scottish writer produced one of the great bestsellers of the Victorian age (named after the reign of Queen Victoria, 1837-1901) entitled *Self Help*. *Self Help* addressed people like Paxton when it stated, "The spirit of self-help is the root of all genuine growth in the individual; and, exhibited in the lives of the many, it constitutes the true source of national vigour and strength." Conversely, most middle-class Britons regarded poverty among able-bodied workers as a moral failing.

"LIKE A THAWING ICEBERG"

By the time of the Crystal Palace exhibition in 1851 the Industrial Revolution had clearly brought greater prosperity and rising standards of living. However, not everyone had benefited equally with the passage of time. Around 1810 some 10 percent of all families earned 100 pounds per year. Those families got about 40 percent of the total national income, while rich families, about half of one percent, got 17 percent. In 1867 wealth was more concentrated: The 10 percent of all families that received 100 pounds per year got about 50 percent of the total national income (an increase of one-quarter), while the small fraction of rich families got 26 percent (an increase of almost one-half).

Below left: Before the Industrial Revolution many lower-class workers supplemented their incomes by home manufacture, or cottage industry. Home manufacture continued, but factory production steadily replaced it. A home worker producing warp yarn without the aid of machinery.

Not only was the gap between the very wealthy and the very poor widening, but some of the economic and social changes had left some people much poorer than they had been in preindustrial times. Consequently, the laboring poor, those whom the Industrial Revolution had bypassed and those who had been squeezed by mechanization, held a very different view than the upper classes about the state of the nation.

Furthermore, industrial change had penetrated unevenly. The most dramatic changes occurred in only five sectors: manufacturing, mining, building, transport, and trade. Between 1800 and 1860 about half of Great Britain's economic resources went into these sectors. Yet even within these most "modern" sectors the old, traditional way of doing things persisted in many areas.

For example, home workers continued their labors, most notably around the industrial centers of northern England, but their contribution to overall productivity was much reduced. Numerous other workers, and particularly women, labored in "the sweating trades" as seamstresses, box or paper bag makers, toy makers, and a host of other crafts still organized on the workshop basis.

Nationwide, only about 30 percent of the labor force worked in activities that had radically changed since the start of the Industrial Revolution. As one historian observed, "Britain was not in 1861 a cotton mill."

Agricultural work remained the single biggest occupation, and agricultural laborers had not shared many of the benefits flowing from the Industrial Revolution. Excluding agricultural workers, most of the labor force remained engaged in old-style industries such as tailoring and shoemaking. As many people worked as domestic servants as worked in the textile industries. More people worked as blacksmiths than as ironworkers.

A keen-eyed writer observed in 1847 that England "exists, like the thawing iceberg, in a transition state."

Below: The astonishing array of new inventions that led to the mechanization of industry gave capitalists unprecedented opportunity. They responded by rapidly concentrating capital and labor in factories. A warping mill.

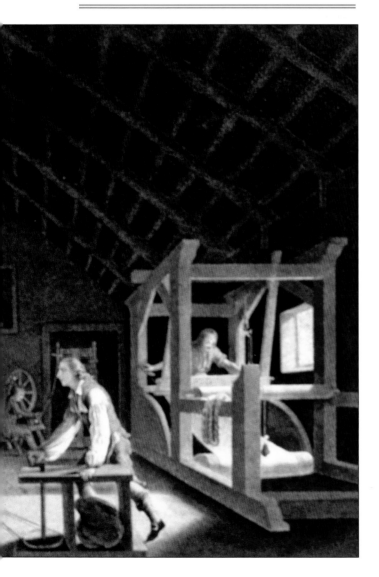

THE RISE OF TRADE UNIONS IN GREAT BRITAIN

In 1819, at St. Peter's Fields, Manchester, a large crowd of working-class people gathered to demand various social reforms. The local militia attacked, killing 11 and wounding 400, including over 100 girls and women. The government thanked the soldiers. The workers called the action "Peterloo," a mocking reference to Wellington's great victory over the French at Waterloo four years earlier.

Trade unions dated back to the thirteenth century. To avoid persecution, unions often disguised themselves as some sort of friendly society or association of like-minded workers. For example, in the woolen industry wool combers, weavers, and stockingers all formed workers' associations. Such associations tried to represent their workers by making collective agreements about wages and the like with the owners. In the late 1700s and again in 1800 Parliament passed acts that made illegal almost all collective working-class activity. These laws drove trade unions underground.

The abuses of the Industrial Revolution combined with economic downturns to bring trade unions back to the surface. Workers hoped to use union organization to counter the power of employers to set working conditions.

ROBERT OWEN

In addition, from time to time social reformers became the champions of the working class. Among them was Robert Owen, who worked to establish a "new moral world" in which laborers would join together to improve their lives. Owen's utopian doctrine provided inspiration for the founding of a host of new labor organizations (Utopia was an imaginary island having a perfect political and social system). Self-help societies, cooperative stores for laborers, plans for cooperative ownership of industrial facilities, and much else sprung up in working-class districts.

In 1827 carpenters formed the first national union in England. Thereafter, some union leaders tried to build a national organization to represent working-class people. John Doherty led the way in 1829 when he founded a "Grand General Union of All the Operative Spinners of the United Kingdom." Owen contributed by forming a "Grand National Moral Union of the Productive Classes of Great Britain and Ireland." Its purpose was to end capitalism and substitute a cooperative system controlled by workers. In other words, Owen and his like were preaching a version of socialism—socialism strictly defined is a form of political

TRANSPORTATION: forced removal from Great Britain to one of its colonies, a sentence inflicted on people convicted of breaking the law

CHARTER: a document setting out the rules for operating an organization

Unions in America:
See also
Volume 10 pages 28–29

economy that puts the means of production and distribution in government hands.

The plans of Owen and others collapsed from internal bickering and stiff opposition from capitalists and the government. For example, in one case the government cruelly sentenced farm laborers to seven years' **transportation** overseas because they had administered oaths, a banned activity, during their enrollment ceremonies. With hindsight it could be seen that Owen and other labor leaders who promoted idealistic trade unionism tried to change too much too fast. But Owen's vision gave the labor movement a sense of unity and a belief in ideals that served it well during the decades of struggle to come.

THE CHARTIST MOVEMENT

In 1838 a London radical, William Lovett, drafted a bill for the reform of Parliament known as "the People's **Charter**." It made

ROBERT OWEN, REFORMER

At the age of 10 the Welsh-born Robert Owen became an apprentice to a clothier. The clothier had a fine library, and the young boy spent much of his time reading. Owen proved a very able businessman and by age 19 was superintendent of a large Manchester cotton mill. He convinced his partners to buy the New Lanark mills, which were located in a Scottish town of 2,000 that included 500 children from the poorhouses and charities of Scottish cities.

By personal example Owen "encouraged the people in habits of order, cleanliness, and thrift." He devoted special attention to educating the young. In 1813 Owen reorganized the mills in order to pursue his vision of how mankind should operate. Owen believed that the great secret to the proper formation of a person's character was to educate him correctly at a very early age. He ran his mills profitably while providing industrial and social welfare programs.

Robert Owen was virtually alone in his support of trade unions and their goals. Many well-to-do Britons believed that shorter factory workdays and higher wages would destroy the entire national economy by making British goods too expensive to compete with those of other nations. One wrote in 1835 about "the vast evils which mischievous cabals among the operatives may inflict on mill-owners, as well as on the commerce of the country." However, the New Lanark mills (below right) flourished under Owen's leadership.

Owen also wrote essays on his philosophy of social reform. His mills at New Lanark "became a place of pilgrimage for social reformers, statesmen, and royal personages." Everyone who visited reported that the children brought up in Owen's system were healthy and happy. His mills subjected adults workers to far less factory discipline than elsewhere. Drunkenness was the only misdemeanor that led to automatic dismissal.

In 1815 Owen began working for factory reform nationwide. He argued that the competition of human labor with machines was a permanent cause of distress. At the same time, Owen sponsored or encouraged "utopian" communities, including New Harmony, Indiana, in America. Numerous labor organizations formed in both Great Britain and the United States to follow Owen's ideals. Owen himself became a leader in the trade union movement.

However, his influence faded for a variety of reasons, including opposition from industrialists and the government as well as Owen's declared hostility to all forms of organized religion. In his old age someone asked him how many people, after he died, would put into practice his views. Owen replied, "Not one."

SUFFRAGE: the right to vote

six demands: universal male **suffrage**; equal electoral districts; vote by ballot; annually elected Parliaments; payment of Parliamentary members (so nonwealthy people could afford to serve in Parliament); and the end of property qualifications for membership in Parliament. The People's Charter gave rise to a working-class movement known as "Chartism."

In February the folowing year a Chartist convention gathered in London to draft a petition to Parliament. It threatened stern measures if Parliament ignored the petition, but the delegates could not agree about what those measures should be. The convention moved to Birmingham in May, and worker riots broke out. This led to the arrest of moderate leaders as well as Lovett.

When the Chartists presented their petition, Parliament quickly rejected it. An armed uprising of Chartists took place later in the year, but authorities quickly suppressed it. The leaders were banished to Australia, and Chartist activists everywhere were arrested and received short prison terms.

The Chartists rallied and learned from their mistakes. They organized more efficiently and three years later submitted the petition again, but this time it had three million signatures. Again Parliament quickly rejected it.

In the late 1840s the national economy improved, and the Chartist movement lost some of its mass support. The 1848 revolutions in continental Europe coupled with a bad harvest

Chartists carried banners calling for "Vote by Ballot," "Universal Suffrage," and "No Qualification" at their demonstrations.

in England stimulated the Chartists to present the petition a third time, which Parliament again rejected.

Although Chartism lingered for another ten years, its appeal waned in the face of general prosperity. However, many labor leaders began their careers during the Chartist debates and continued to serve a variety of working-class causes. As was the case with Robert Owen, Chartist ideals provided inspiration for future reform movements long after the Chartist organization ended.

Because of the failures associated with efforts to organize national unions, until the 1870s most unions remained small and regional. As the Manchester Stonemasons noted, "Past experience had taught us that we have had general [national] union enough."

The Chartists understood that members of Parliament (left) lived in a different world from the working class.

THE BRITISH WORKING CLASS

In Great Britain most complaints about capitalism focused on the sufferings inflicted by capitalism on the workers. One frequent source of complaint was the imposition of factory discipline.

FACTORY DISCIPLINE

For decades preceding the Industrial Revolution cottage industry workers had established their own family work discipline. Typically the family goal was to finish their work by Saturday in time, for example, for the clothier to collect the spun yarn. The family did not work during the weekend and often took Monday off as well, blessing this privilege by calling it "Saint Monday."

One important consequence of the expanding use of machines was the introduction of factory discipline. Workers' freedom to organize their own time declined dramatically. Instead, the machine set the pace of work, and all workers had to do their part regularly and well.

To ensure factory discipline, factory owners established penalties for latecomers and for careless and lazy workers. A list of fines in one cotton mill was typical:

	Fine		Reason
	shilling	pence	
Any spinner found with his window open	1	0	windows maintained humidity closed
Dirty at his work	1	0	
Washing himself	1	0	wasting time
Leaving his oil can out of its place	6	0	inefficient
Spinning with gas light too long in the morning	2	0	wasting valuable gas
Heard whistling	1	0	
Being five minutes after the last bell rings	2	0	
Two spinners found together in necessary [lavatory], each	1	0	questionable morality

SHILLING: a unit of British money, a silver coin equal to a certain number of pence

PENCE: plural of penny, a unit of British money

Factory rules in America:
See also
Volume 5 page 51

Writers far removed from the working class argued that factory work was good for children's health: "There are no trades in which young persons are engaged in numbers, such as sewing, pin-making, or coal-mining, nearly so salubrious [healthful], or so comfortable as a cotton-mill."

The heaviest fine, six **shillings**, was for sick workers who stayed home and failed to find a replacement. The penalty supposedly paid for the cost of the wasted steam that went unused because of the worker's absence.

Women and children made up almost 70 percent of the factory workforce. In 1835 cotton mills in one county employed 246 eleven-year-old boys and 155 eleven-year-old girls at weekly wages of two shillings 3.5 **pence** and 2 shillings 4.75 pence respectively. In the age group 11-16 the mills employed 1,169 boys whose average weekly wage was 4 shillings 1.75 pence and 1,123 girls at 4 shillings 3 pence. This age group contributed more workers than any other. The 612 young men aged 21 to 26 earned roughly twice as much as the 780 women in the same age group. Even though they were paid less then men, the women's wages still were higher than the cost of living. In other words, they earned a "living wage."

WHAT A LIVING WAGE MEANT

A working-class English family in 1833 with five children lived on the husband's wages as a spinner. Since the age of eleven the eldest daughter had contributed by providing about 20 percent of the family's income working as her father's piecer. The family did not go hungry, although they hardly ate well:

"Breakfast is generally porridge, bread, and milk, lined with flour or oatmeal. On Sunday, a cup of tea and bread and butter. Dinner, on weekdays, potatoes and bacon, and bread, which is generally white. On Sunday a little flesh meat; no butter, egg, or pudding. Teatime every day, tea and bread and butter; nothing extra on Sunday at tea. Supper, oatmeal porridge and milk; sometimes potato and milk. Sundays, sometimes a little bread and cheese for supper; never have this on weekdays. Now and then buy eggs when they are [inexpensive]....They never taste any other vegetable than potatoes."

In other words, this family ate the same unbalanced, monotonous meals day after day, week after week.

"The house consists of four rooms, two on each floor; the furniture consists of two beds in the same room, one for themselves and the other for the children; have four chairs, one table in the house, boxes to put clothes into, no chest of drawers, two pans and a tea-kettle for boiling, a gridiron and frying-pan, half a dozen large and small plates, four pairs of knives and forks, several pewter spoons."

These possessions were all their worldly goods.

"Two of the children go to school at 3 pence a week each; they are taught reading for this, but not writing. Have a few books, such as Bible, hymn-book, and several small books that the children have got as prizes at the Sunday school."

In other words, the family was barely literate, and the purpose of the little education the children received was to be able to study religion and read the Bible.

Such was the material world that a "living wage" provided in an English home during the Industrial Revolution.

LIVING AT THE BOTTOM

While the Industrial Revolution brought enormous gains for many, it also brought pain. The two largest groups who did not benefit were agricultural laborers and skilled workers who were displaced by machinery. The former suffered badly between 1780 and 1850. From 1795 to 1820 the price of white bread doubled, indicating a doubling in the cost of living, while their average wage went up only 12%. Perhaps worse were the experiences of skilled workers such as handloom weavers, framework knitters, wool combers, and calico printers who simply could not compete with machine-made, mass-produced goods. Their standard of living declined by every measure.

Typical was the experience of a tailor who had belonged to a trade society of fellow workers (almost a trade union). For fifteen years during the opening decades of the nineteenth century he had worked profitably: "I was seldom out of work...no one could have been happier than I was." However, as his sight failed, he no longer could get regular work, so he switched to a shop that made cheap clothes. This removed him from the trade society.

He and six others labored long hours in a tiny workshop where he earned half as much money as before: "I am convinced I lost my eyesight by working in that cheap shop....It is by the ruin of such men as me that these masters are enabled to undersell the better shops....That's the way, sir, the cheap clothes is produced, by making blind beggars of the workmen, like myself, and throwing us on the parish [church charity] in our old age."

The tailor had worked in what was called "the sweating trades" (in America, "sweatshops"). Laborers in the sweating trades worked long hours for low wages to manufacture basic, low-quality goods for the mass market in an effort to compete

As home production on hand looms gave way to factory production on mechanized looms, cotton weavers sang the song:

"Come all you cotton weavers, your looms you may pull down.
You must get employed in factories, in country or in town,
For our cotton masters have found out a wonderful scheme,
Their calico goods now wove by hand they're going to weave by steam."

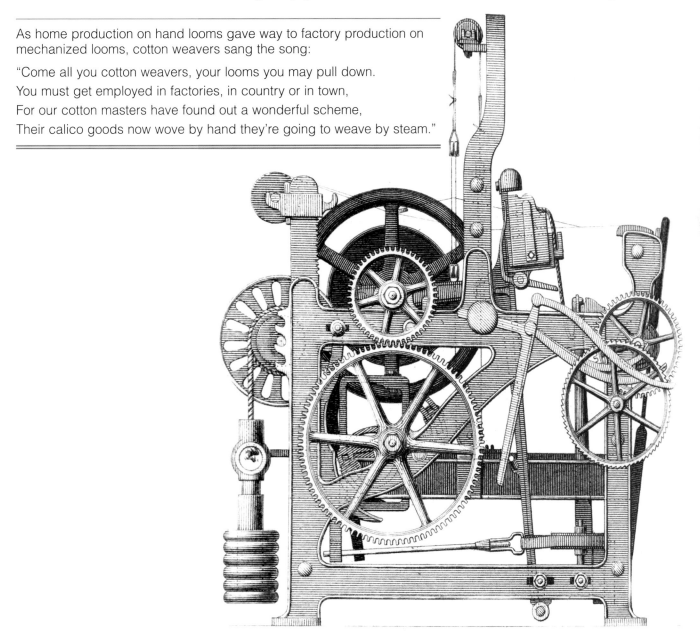

During the 1830s two British writers, Professor Andrew Ure and Dr. James Kay, expressed opposing views of machine-driven factory work:

Ure believed that "The labour is not incessant in a power-driven factory…because it is performed in partnership with the workman's never failing friend, the steam-engine."

Kay argued that "While the engine runs the people must work   men, women and children yoked together with iron and steam...subject to a thousand sources of suffering…chained fast to the iron machine which knows no suffering and no weariness."

SWEATED TRADES: trades in which workers endure long hours, low pay, and poor working conditions

with factory manufacture. A historian of the Industrial Revolution observed that the era "witnessed massive expansion both of the **sweated trades** and of under-paid and exploited casual labor."

TWO VIEWS OF THE LABORING CLASS

A Glasgow professor named Andrew Ure had a keen interest in the impact of manufacturing advances on workers. In 1835 he published his conclusions on working-class conditions inside factories. Ure visited factories and observed what took place. He wrote that he never saw child laborers being abused. He also argued against the view that "the unceasing motion of the steam-engine" forced workers to work too hard in excessively tedious labor: "In an establishment for spinning or weaving cotton, all the hard work is performed by the steam-engine, which leaves for the attendant no hard labor at all, and literally nothing to do in general; but at intervals to perform some delicate operation." Ure calculated that for at least 45 seconds out of each minute workers stood idle. Thus a child who worked a typical 12-hour day actually had nine hours of inaction.

Ure contrasted this labor with other occupations such as stone masonry or carpentry where workers had to perform hard physical labor for at least ten hours a day. He came away convinced that the factory system benefited workers and that their protests against it were slowing the rate at which workers improved their lives. He considered the transition from cottage industry to factory and noted that "when the handicraftsman exchanges hard work with fluctuating employment and pay, for continuous work of a lighter kind with steady wages, he must necessarily renounce his old prerogative of stopping when he pleases because he would thereby throw the whole establishment into disorder." Ure concluded that "The factory system...instead of being detrimental to the comfort of the laboring population, is its grand Palladium [protector]."

Like Ure, James Kay, a Manchester physician, saw the benefits of industrialization in spreading prosperity. Unlike Ure, Kay also saw the hardships and squalor that surrounded many factory workers: "The population employed in the cotton factories rises at five o'clock in the morning, works in the mills from six till eight o'clock, and returns home for half an hour or forty minutes for breakfast." Breakfast consisted of tea or coffee with a little bread. Workers then returned to the mills until noon, at which time they came back home for another meal: "Amongst those who obtain the lowest rates of wages this meal generally consists of boiled potatoes." At one o'clock

CHILD LABOR IN GREAT BRITAIN

Lower-class children had always been expected to work. In preindustrial times children contributed to their family's income by working in the cottage industries and on the farm. Parents or older siblings directed young children in such tasks as carding, sorting, and spinning. In the fields children could plant, weed, tend the crops and animals, and assist during harvest. The work children contributed often made a crucial economic difference in how well a family lived.

When the Industrial Revolution caused manufacturing to shift from the cottage to the factory, it seemed perfectly natural to almost everyone that children should work in the factory. Instead of having parents supervise their work, a master or a foreman imposed discipline while machines set the pace of work. Consequently, children had to work harder and for longer hours. Some unscrupulous factories particularly welcomed orphaned children and paupers because they either had no parents or their parents were powerless to interfere with the orders set by the foremen.

Few Britons thought that the government had any right to regulate the relationship between parents and children. Moreover, many

In 1835 a doctor observing children working in textile mills reported, "I feel convinced that...the long confinement in mills, the want of rest, the shameful reduction of the intervals for meals, and especially the premature working of children, greatly reduce the health and vigour, and account for the wretched appearance of the operatives."

Not everyone was so concerned about the well-being of working children. While some observers expressed misgivings about the hardships endured by children working in factories, others made such statements as, "It is scarcely possible for any employment to be lighter."

Child labor in America:
See also
Volume 10 pages 18–21

asserted that the nation's prosperity depended on child labor. They argued that Great Britain's population had grown so large that it could no longer feed itself. Manufacturing profits paid for imported food. Manufacturing depended on capital, while capital relied on profits. Child labor allowed manufacturers to keep their mills running long hours and thus earn profits. As one historian observed, "This was the circle in which the nation found its conscience entangled."

Certain facts supported this view. Almost half of all Britons in 1821 were under the age of 20, so young people made up an important percentage of the labor pool. Not only was child labor plentiful, it was cheap. Children in general earned between one-third and one-sixth what adults earned. Child workers were more docile than adults and thus more easily broken to factory discipline. Thus factory owners had every incentive to employ children.

they returned to work until seven o'clock or later and came back home for another meal like breakfast or lunch.

Kay wrote that this malnourished population crowded "into one dense mass, in cottages separated by narrow, unpaved, and almost pestilential streets; in an atmosphere loaded with the smoke and exhalations of a large manufacturing city." Likewise, the air that they breathed during their 12-hour workday was "loaded with dust or filaments of cotton, and impure from constant respiration, or from other causes."

Kay concluded that the workers were like animals, mere "drudges who watch the movements, and assist the operations, of a mighty material force, which toils with an energy ever unconscious of fatigue."

Andrew Ure and James Kay: Two highly educated men looked at the same conditions and saw two very different things.

Professor Ure argued that factory workers had easier jobs than tradesmen such as carpenters because the tradesmen served long apprenticeships, had to acquire tools, and had to use their muscles continuously.

Opposite: A British cartoonist in 1850 expressed a commonly held view that American slaves lived easier lives than British factory workers.

24

BRITISH SOCIETY WEIGHS THE COST OF REFORM

Since Elizabethan times England had a system of relief for those who could not help themselves and employment for those who could work but were not doing so. Accordingly, "workhouses" or "houses of industry" existed for the unemployed poor in both rural areas and towns. England also had a body of laws, the "Poor Law," designed to provide relief for the aged, sick, and infant poor as well as work for the able-

Parliament first passed a law to permit the establishment of workhouses in 1723. The only assistance offered to the poverty-stricken was room and board (meals) in a workhouse in exchange for their labor. Within ten years at least a hundred workhouses existed in the London area alone.

bodied in workhouses. In the late 1700s an additional measure, the so-called Speenhamland system, supplemented the Poor Law. This system gave allowances to workers whose wages were below what was considered a subsistence level, or living wage.

Although well-intended, the consequence was an enormous fourfold increase in the cost of public relief in under forty years. The property owners whose taxes paid for the Poor Law protested. In 1834 Parliament responded by passing a new Poor Law that was much harsher. In keeping with the middle-class view that poverty among able-bodied workers was a sign of moral failing, the new law provided no relief for such workers except the workhouse. Since workhouse conditions were typically awful, the idea was that this measure would compel the poor to seek regular work.

PARTIAL REFORM

Some politicians and industrialists believed that among the working poor, at least the orphans and paupers needed some protection. Robert Peel—a mill owner who was elected to

Parliament—became the leader of this campaign. As a result Parliament passed an act in 1802 that limited the working day for pauper apprentice children to twelve hours and forbade them from doing nightwork. Other measures included providing a new suit of clothes once a year, separate sleeping quarters for boys and girls with not more than two children per bed, and monthly attendance at church. Any factory that employed pauper children had to register with local authorities. Parliament empowered the authorities to see that the factories obeyed the law. It is notable that at this time pauper apprentices made up only a small percentage of the total number of child laborers, so the improvements, such as they were, applied only to a small segment of the child laborer population.

Largely because of the effort of social reformer Robert Owen, in 1819 Parliament extended the terms of the 1802 act to all children. Furthermore, Parliament forbade employing children under the age of nine. However, Parliament appointed only two inspectors for the entire country. With so few inspectors abusive factory owners knew that there was little chance they would be caught. Indeed, over a ten-year period inspectors prosecuted only two factories for failing to obey the child labor rules.

Parliament passed a new Factory Act in 1833 to protect child labor. This time it appointed four inspectors and limited their inspections to the

Top: Manufacturers took advantage of workhouses by arranging to support the inmates in exchange for their forced labor. Under such arrangements workhouses resembled prisons. Some employers cruelly chained workhouse children to prevent them from running away. Workhouse inmates.

Left: Robert Peel fought an uphill battle to pass laws protecting working children. Opponents made numerous and varied arguments against such legislation: The laws would actually harm children, their families would suffer from the loss of children's wages, and parents would be unable to afford school for their nonworking children anyway. Worst of all, factories would be unable to function without their youngest workers, so the national economy would suffer.

textile industry. Not only was this far too few inspectors, but the act ignored working conditions in mines, ironworks, brickyards, and other places where children commonly labored. This failure of the government meant that children continued to work at dangerous, low-paying, uncomfortable, and dirty jobs well into the 1860s. In addition, the acts did nothing for adult workers.

Children in American coal mines:
See also
Volume 10 pages 18–19 and 22–23

CHILDREN UNDERGROUND

England's Industrial Revolution had created a tremendous demand for coal. Mine owners exploited child workers, particularly orphans, to work underground six days a week for 12 to 18 hours a day. Work conditions were terrible, with heat so intense it melted candles and air so foul and dirty that the children sometimes could not even eat. As a consequence, the children grew up weak and physically deformed.

In 1842 Parliament banned the underground (mining) employment of children and women. This did away with one of the great abuses of the industrial age. Yet for many families it proved an economic disaster because, as bad as conditions were, poor mining families depended on income from women and children to survive. Two years later Parliament passed another important act that established the half-time system for children and gave women and young adults the 12-hour day. However, this act only applied to the textile industry. Reform in other industries waited until the second half of the century.

In the mid-1800s men, women, and children as young as seven still worked as beasts of burden in coal mines. Hitched to tubs of coal with a device called "the painful harness," they dragged and pushed the tubs through low, wet passageways.

Nonetheless, the relief provided by the Act of 1844 did improve conditions and set a precedent that was later followed both in Great Britain and in other countries.

Eventually, two trends converged to change western society's view of child labor: Improvements in the machines themselves substituted automatic controls for the type of industrial tasks children had formerly performed, and growing numbers of reformers condemned the cruelty of industrial child labor. One gradual effect of the Industrial Revolution was to take children out of the labor pool. Instead of having children contribute to a family's income, the main task of childhood became education. Over time (in the 1830s in the northern United States, in the 1870s in Germany and France, in 1880 in Great Britain) compulsory primary school education became the legal mandate.

PARLIAMENT RESPONDS:
THE GROWTH OF GOVERNMENT

1802: Health and Morals of Apprentices Act – Limits the workday of pauper apprentices to 12 hours. Local justices of the peace may inspect textile mills.

1819: Peel's Factory Act (cotton mills only) – Cotton mills may not employ children under the age of nine. Workday for children 9-16 years limited to 12 hours. No inspectors to enforce new laws.

1833: Factory Act – 1819 act extended to all textile mills except silk and lace. In addition, children aged 9 to 13 limited to 8-hour workday, 13 to18 a 12-hour workday. Children under 13 must receive education for 2 hours per workday, paid for by the worker. Four factory inspectors appointed for entire nation.

1842: Mines Act – Women and girls prohibited from underground work; boys under age of 10 likewise. National inspectorate created.

1844: Factory Act (textile mills only) – Workday for children aged 8 to 13 limited to 6.5 hours per day. Children to receive minimum of 3 hours of education per day. Women forbidden nightwork and limited to 12 hours work per 24.

1847: Factory Act – Workday for women and children aged 13 to 18 limited to 10 hours per day or 58 hours per week.

1853: Employment of Children in Factories Act – Children aged 8 to 13 cannot begin work before 6 a.m. or after 6 p.m. or 2 p.m. on Saturday.

1867: Factory Act Extension Act and Hours of Labour Regulation Act – Earlier factory legislation extended to include nontextile factories and workshops. Prohibits employing children under age of 8. Children aged 8 to 13 years must receive minimum of 10 hours of education per week.

1867: Agricultural Gangs Act – Prohibits employment of children under age 8 and employment of women and children in a field gang that includes men.

THE INDUSTRIAL REVOLUTION AND OPPOSING VIEWS OF ECONOMIC PHILOSOPHY

As the Industrial Revolution changed society and the lives of workers, the thinkers of the era developed theories about how industrial economies should work. Three of them—Adam Smith, Friedrich Engels, and Karl Marx—wrote groundbreaking books that set forth for the first time the opposing principles of capitalism and communism.

Born in Scotland in 1723, at age 14 Adam Smith attended the University of Glasgow, where he studied moral philosophy. He subsequently went to Oxford University and then took up the subject of "the progress of opulence [wealth]." While in his mid-twenties, he began to develop an economic philosophy of "the obvious and simple system of natural liberty." He received an appointment back in Glasgow as a professor of logic and later of

Adam Smith (right) believed in free trade, arguing that the government should not tax imports but let buyers decide whether they preferred to buy foreign or domestic goods.

moral philosophy. Among his works during this period was a book on human nature, *The Theory of Moral Sentiments*.

In 1767, as the Industrial Revolution began to explode around him, Smith started work on a nine-year labor that led to his best-known book, *An Inquiry into the Nature and Causes of the Wealth of Nations*. Published in 1776 (the year of revolution in America), *The Wealth of Nations* (as it is remembered) was the first major study of what is called laissez-faire economics. This term comes from the French meaning "let people do as they please."

Smith also believed that capitalism, coupled with the freedom to accumulate wealth with little government interference, would create jobs and thus bring more wealth to more people. Well-dressed capitalists gather at the Royal Exchange in London.

GUILD: medieval form of trade association, whereby skilled workers in the same craft or trade organized to protect their business interests

In Smith's view the perfect system of liberty flowed from market-determined (instead of **guild**-regulated) wages and free instead of government-regulated enterprise. He described the evolution of society toward commercial interdependence, introducing the phrase "the invisible hand." Smith understood "the invisible hand" to be the effect of the decisions of thousands of competing individuals acting in their self-interest. He explained how "the invisible hand" guided the economy. Smith thus portrayed the free market as a self-correcting system. He asserted that the combined effect of the individual drives toward self-betterment would grow the economy. But the wealth of nations would increase only if free competition reigned and if governments did not inhibit economic growth by listening to the pleas of businessmen who asked for special privilege.

Even though the impact of the Industrial Revolution was apparent at a great iron works within a few miles of where Smith wrote, he had little to say about industrialization. Nonetheless, Adam Smith laid much of the intellectual basis for capitalism. Whereas socialism saw class struggle as the driving force behind social evolution, Smith saw "human nature" motivated by the desire for self-betterment as the driving force.

Before his death Smith apparently contributed a large amount of his own wealth to charity. Simultaneously, in the tradition of the times he destroyed nearly all of his manuscripts. Only one portrait of him survives along with a statement to a friend: "I am a beau [handsome] in nothing but my books."

FRIEDRICH ENGELS

Friedrich Engels grew up in a middle-class German family. His father owned a textile factory in Germany and was a

Right: Friedrich Engels described children returning home after a day of work in the coal mines and collapsing on the floor to "fall asleep at once, without being able to take a bite of food, and have to be washed and put to bed while asleep....It seems a universal practice among these children to spend Sunday in bed to recover in some degree from the overexertion of the week."

An orphan boy living in a workhouse and sent to work in a cotton mill became "so weary of confinement, he would have gladly exchanged situations with the poorest of the poor children whom, from the upper windows of the workhouse, he had seen begging from door to door, offering matches for sale."

partner in a cotton factory in Manchester. At the age of 18 he developed an interest in liberal and revolutionary German philosophy. He lived in England from 1842 to 1844, where he served as an effective businessman while simultaneously pursuing his real interests by writing articles on communism.

He read parliamentary reports on English economic and political conditions, met with workers and radical leaders, and gathered material for a book about the rise of industry in England and the resultant wretched working conditions. The book, *The Conditions of the Working Class in England in 1844*, became a classic in its field.

Engels described three awful cases of London poverty. He then added: "It is not, of course, suggested that all London workers are so poverty-stricken as these three families. There can be no doubt that for every worker who is rendered utterly destitute by society there are ten who are better off. On the other hand it can be confidently asserted that thousands of decent and industrious families...live under truly deplorable conditions which are an affront to human dignity. It is equally incontestable that every working man without exception may well suffer a similar fate through no fault of his own and despite all his efforts to keep his head above water."

His experiences led Engels to the conclusion that the existing system of private property would lead to a world made up of "millionaires and paupers." He believed that this inequality would lead to revolution and the subsequent end of private property.

In 1844 Engels met a man who was to become one of modern history's most influential economic thinkers, Karl Marx. Four years later, in 1848, they coauthored the *Communist Manifesto*. Marx had to flee his home in Germany and spent the rest of his life in Great Britain. There Engels showed him firsthand the social and economic problems caused by the Industrial Revolution.

Marx's observations and his book study led him to conclude that capitalism was merely a stage in society's evolution. He predicted that as industrial society developed, there would be inevitable conflict between capital (whose goal was profit) and labor (whose work generated profit for the capitalists). The conflict would result in the triumph of the majority, namely, the workers, and a classless society would emerge.

Engels became Marx's closest collaborator and edited the second and third volumes of *Das Kapital* (Capital) after Marx's death. The two men laid down the foundation of modern communism.

Karl Marx argued in his *Communist Manifesto* that under capitalism the worker "becomes an appendage of the machine."

THE BARRACKS OF INDUSTRY

By 1850, for the first time in history a large state, Great Britain, had half its population living in towns. The rapid urbanization of the country was taking place in the absence of governmental regulation.

THE PROBLEMS OF URBANIZATION

Throughout most of the Industrial Revolution great wealth and great poverty had existed side by side. The novelist Charles Dickens described a working-class neighborhood in his 1854 book *Hard Times*. He based his fictional "Coketown" on Preston, a major factory town:

Urbanization in America:
See also
Volume 10 pages 43–54

"It was a town of red brick, or of brick that would have been red if smoke and ashes had allowed it; but as matters stood it was a town of unnatural red and black like the painted face of a savage. It was a town of machinery and tall chimneys, out of which interminable serpents of smoke trailed themselves for ever and ever....It had a black canal in it [black from water pollution] and a river that ran purple with ill-smelling dye, and vast piles of buildings full of windows where there was a rattling and trembling all day long, and where the pistons of the steam-engine worked monotonously up and down like the head of an elephant in a state of melancholy madness."

In this polluted, noisy environment the factory workers lived in identical houses and "all went in and out at the same hours...to do the same work, and to whom every day was the same as yesterday and tomorrow, and every year the counterpart of the last and the next."

Everywhere the rising middle class moved away from working-class neighborhoods like Preston in order to live in better conditions. In England, for example, middle-class suburbs developed on the western outskirts of industrial towns

An idealized view of Preston, Charles Dickens's inspiration for "Coketown."

and cities so the prevailing winds would not blow the smells of the factories and slums in their direction! While the more wealthy could make sure that their taxes went for improved paving, lighting, water supplies, and similar public utilities, the lower-class city dwellers had to tolerate bad housing, foul water, and general filth.

In 1844 a special commission assigned the task of investigating the "Health of Towns" reported on the condition of workers' homes near Preston. The factory workers lived in a crowded set of cottages separated by little backyards on land that had recently been pasture. An open sewer ran the entire length of the street.

Conditions in urban areas were much worse. The new industrial centers witnessed a steady influx of people whom the factory owners housed as cheaply as possible. No controls existed to regulate dumping trash or even how to dispose of human waste. A health inspector in Manchester reported that the privies (outhouses) were "inaccessible from filth and numbering only two to 250 people." The sewage system was usually on the surface, so waste flowed along open ditches and street gutters. Cesspools with open grids stood next to front doors. Drinking-water supplies were unclean, and no one worried about water pollution in streams and rivers. Cemeteries, slaughterhouses, tanneries, and industries of all sorts contributed their effluent both as water and air pollutants. Since the crowded buildings blocked air flow, the stench outside was horrible. Indoors in winter, when houses were tightly sealed to keep the inhabitants warm, foul smells from human waste, unwashed bodies, and cooking filled the home.

The living conditions were more than simply unpleasant, they were deadly. Workers suffered chronic diseases such as dysentery. Contagious diseases spread easily in the crowded conditions with children suffering the most. As late as 1860 about 26 of every 100 children living in working-class neighborhoods died before the age of five. Infant mortality in 1870 remained high, with three children in 20 failing to live until the age of one.

Government commissioners reported that the houses of the poor had "no yard, no privy, and no receptacle for refuse. Consequently the narrow, unpaved streets, in which mud and water stagnate, become the common receptacle of offal and ordure." During the same period an upper-class writer claimed that thousands of British mill workers, assisted by their children's mill wages, "eat meat every day, wear broadcloth on the Sunday, dress their wives and children well, furnish their houses with mahogany and carpets, subscribe to publications, and pass through life with much of humble respectability."

Making things worse was the destruction of many old city centers to clear the way for new businesses and industry. New railway lines and stations, warehouses, and office buildings replaced homes and forced the poor to relocate. In a typical case the Scottish city of Glasgow saw 20,000 poor displaced from the city center as a result of railway construction alone. Between 1830 and 1880 about 100,000 poor Londoners had to move to make way for "progress." Behind the facade of new urban structures Victorian cities remained very unhealthy places to live for most inhabitants. In the words of one historian the "problems of arranging and controlling the expansion of the towns was thus the most urgent of the problems created by the Industrial Revolution."

Below: In the days before cities began piping water into working-class homes, city dwellers either carried water from public pumps or purchased it from water carriers. Although an indoor water supply was more convenient, it was rarely clean and safe to drink. A waterworks on the edge of London drew water from the polluted river.

Above: A reporter who visited Leeds in 1845 wrote that "the smoke and fumes arising from the various works" made the houses of the working people "most unhealthy." Added to the polluted air was the stench of "ashes, garbage, and filth of all kinds...thrown from the doors and windows of the houses upon the surface of the streets" and outhouses that were not cleaned for six months at a time.

THE RESPONSE OF GOVERNMENT

In 1840 a Parliamentary committee observed that there was no general building law in force for the entire country, although "one of the first duties of a humane government" should be to provide decent shelter for the entire population. In one working-class district in Manchester the homes were built on swamp land and frequently flooded. And even tiny, ten-foot-square cellars housed ten or more workers. The committee made numerous recommendations, including a general building law, the establishment of a board of health in all towns, and the banning of cellar dwellings and back-to-back houses. Yet Parliament failed to act.

Meanwhile, individual cities could enact local legislation.

Because of the terrible public health conditions advisers recommended that Queen Victoria not visit the great industrial cities of Liverpool and Manchester. When she ignored them in 1851, it was "almost a matter of wonder." But consider that the standard of public sanitation was such that even the royal apartments at Buckingham Palace received their "fresh air" via the common sewer line. Queen Victoria leaving the palace to visit the Great Exhibition at Crystal Palace.

Yet local politicians were often no more able to decide what to do than those at the national level. Furthermore, many technical experts, including sanitary engineers, failed to understand the relationship between dirt, overcrowding, and disease. In 1849 an engineer who did grasp this relationship and who promoted sewage pipe drainage conducted an urban inspection. With great effort he convinced some opponents of such drainage to accompany him and reported that they "declared in the strongest terms that they had no idea of the state of things existing around them. But this I have found in every town I have visited; few besides the medical gentlemen know anything of the utter wretchedness and misery produced by want of proper sanitary regulations."

THE MIND OF THE WORKER

Most of society shared an attitude toward the lower classes that work was the only thing they were good for. Adam Smith's observation that while the division of labor was good for production, it was bad for the mind of the worker did not bother them. During the 12-hour workday, as ever more workers performed a monotonous routine, they became increasingly stifled mentally. Outside of work no public provisions existed to stimulate the mind. Neither parks, open spaces, libraries, museums, nor anything else existed to provide leisure and education for the working classes.

Indeed, little provision was made for education of any sort.

In the absence of publicly supported schools or a legal requirement to send children to school education was beyond the reach of most poor children.

A working-class area that had a population of about 100,000 lacked a single public day-school for the poor. One upper-class man spoke for the majority when he dismissed the importance of education. He asserted that the question to ask was not whether education would develop a child's facilities for happiness and citizenship, but whether it "would make him a good servant in agriculture and other laborious employments to which his rank in society has destined him."

The Industrial Revolution brought the urbanization of a nation. The nation's leaders, in turn, were slow to understand and then address the problems caused by urbanization. On the national level Parliament did not adopt town-planning laws until the twentieth century. Until that time urban slums continued to grow, often outside of any regulatory control. In the words of a pair of social critics workers lived in urban areas that were "not the refuge of civilization but the barracks of an industry."

LOOKING TOWARD THE FUTURE

England had given birth to the Industrial Revolution, and there also began many of society's adjustments to the revolution. By the 1870s and 1880s the uneven distribution of wealth was disturbing increasing numbers of people. British attitudes changed from the happy complacency of the previous decades to a new era of constructive social legislation. Ahead lay reforms in education, housing, public health, old age pensions, unemployment, and workmen's compensation.

From 1834 everyone in need of help, such as the unemployed, old, or sick had to go into the workhouses. Families were split up, and the men were forced into unpleasant jobs like crushing bones to make glue, while the women had to clean the workhouse and cook meals. The dining hall in a large workhouse.

THE WORKING CLASS IN FRANCE, GERMANY, AND RUSSIA

FRANCE

Throughout the industrial world governments and society struggled with troubling social issues brought about by the Industrial Revolution. No government or business at the time readily granted working people higher wages or political rights such as the right to organize unions. France was no exception. By any measure France during the period 1830 to 1914 was a leading world power. Yet there, too, industrial workers endured deplorable conditions.

In France the term industrial worker covered a broad range of work. In 1850 small workshops with fewer than 10 employees apiece employed a total of about 2.8 million workers. Such artisans in small workshops represented the largest category of industrial worker. The second largest category comprised village workers who followed the traditional pattern of combining farm work with cottage industry. This group included rural spinners and weavers, village **cutlers** and blacksmiths, and rural charcoal burners. Establishments with more than 10 workers each, officially described as "large-scale," although most were actually merely slightly larger workshops, employed 1.3 million workers.

Regardless of their classification, rural and urban workers had serious complaints about their working conditions. Artisans in small workshops opposed the new machines that threatened their livelihoods. Rural workers in cottage industry, particularly hand-loom weavers, faced falling wages due to competition from machine-made textiles. Factory workers confronted harsh factory discipline. All workers shared complaints about the exploitation of women and children, long

Early industry in France:
See also
Volume 3 pages 44–52

CUTLER: artisan who makes or repairs metal cutting tools, such as knives

A metal-working shop of late eighteenth-century France. Such workshops continued to operate alongside the growing number of factories.

CHILD LABOR IN FRENCH AND BRITISH INDUSTRY

CHILD LABOR IN FRANCE

In the industrial regions of France around 1850 nearly half of the children aged 10 to 15 worked in industry. Two of every three of them worked in the textile industry. Factory owners hired children to do simpler tasks that did not require much training and thus justified paying them a fraction of the wages paid adult workers.

Silk factories in Lyons hired girls as young as twelve and housed them in dormitories on the factory grounds, where women, often nuns, imposed strict discipline, as well as prayer and hymn-singing. A local official wrote in 1852 that the girls' supervisors "prolong their work beyond all limits, even making the young people work whole nights, principally at the time of year when orders are pressing." For this virtual slavery the girls received a bed and meals, and their parents received a small annual payment. Factory owners often required parents to agree to multiyear contracts.

The typical factory workday was at least 12 hours, but in some establishments as long as 16 hours, regardless of the worker's age. The 1841 Factory Law limited children's workdays to 12 hours in only certain types of factories. In 1874 France applied the child labor laws to all industrial establishments and provided for inspectors to enforce the laws. The inspectors could not possibly visit every employer, so many children as young as 10 continued to labor long hours. In 1892 France prohibited the employment of all children under the age of 13.

CHILD LABOR IN BRITISH FACTORIES: EYEWITNESSES

Professor Andrew Ure, an enthusiastic supporter of child labor in factories, argued that the children he observed on factory visits "seemed to be always cheerful and alert, taking pleasure in the light play of their muscles, enjoying the mobility natural to their age. The scene of industry...was always exhilarating....The work of these lively elves seemed to resemble a sport....As to exhaustion by the day's work, they evinced no trace of it on emerging from the mill in the evening; for they immediately began to

skip about...and to commence their little amusements with the same alacrity as boys issuing from a school."

However, workdays of 15 hours or more were common. A cotton mill in Shrewsbury, England, operated from 5 a.m. until 8 or 9 p.m, six days a week. Children who lived some distance from the mill had to leave home early enough to walk to work—even in the dead of winter—and arrive on time. Mill overseers frequently beat late arrivals with a leather strap. Some children were seen by their neighbors to leave their houses at 3 in the morning and not arrive back home until 10 or 11 at night. The children employed there frequently had trouble staying awake on the job.

A young man who had worked at this mill since the age of seven reported in 1831 that if a child grew drowsy at his work, the overseer "walks round the room with a stick in his hand, and he touches that child on the shoulder, and says, 'Come here.' In a corner of the room is an iron cistern [tank]; it is filled with water; he takes this boy, and takes him up by the legs, and dips him over head in the cistern, and sends him to work for the remainder of the day."

Those fortunate enough to escape punishment for their sleepiness might face a worse fate—falling asleep and falling into the clutches of a machine. A witness described a little girl who worked at a spinning machine. As she grew tired, she leaned "against the box with an upright shaft, and the shaft got hold of her clothes, and she was carried round the shaft." The girl "got entangled in the machinery, till all her clothes were tore off her back." Only because her coworker was able to stop the machinery did she escape serious injury. Even so, her boss beat her for being careless.

Right: Parliament held hearings to investigate working conditions, including beatings of children by factory overseers. A witness testified that in his town, "The children are shamefully and most cruelly beaten with a horsewhip, strap, stick, hammer handle, file, or whatever tool is nearest at hand, or are struck with the clenched fist or kicked." The reasons given for beatings included arriving late at work, working too slowly, or talking. Parents were afraid to complain about the beatings because complaints only resulted in worse beatings for their children.

Opposite: Young girls employed as weavers at a British textile mill.

work hours (15-hour workdays with breaks totaling 1.5 hours for meals were typical), poor housing conditions, and their inability to do anything to improve their lot since the government prohibited trade unions and strikes. A writer in the 1840s estimated that one-third of Lille's inhabitants lived in permanent poverty. A Rouen factory owner stated that 60 percent of his employees did not earn a living wage.

A French doctor described some typical dwellings for industrial workers in 1835. He wrote that to enter the homes, he had to go through "an opening like a drain below street level." The sleeping quarters were cold, dark rooms where "Foul water oozes out of the walls." The only furniture was a few shabby beds, a loom, and a spinning wheel. The children were "pale, flabby, and sickly." He sadly noted that "They seem to belong to a different species from the healthy children—so shapely and robust" who played on nearby streets where the more prosperous lived.

WORKER PROTEST

It is not surprising that such conditions led to worker resistance. Simultaneously, French Socialists, who believed that the community or society, not individuals or capitalists, should own the means of production and distribution, thought through these conditions and proposed remedies. When

The poor living standards endured by France's working class weakened the health of their children. As a result, the army typically had to reject almost half of the young conscripts from industrialized areas because of poor health.

workers in Lyons violently took over the city in 1831 and then were crushed by the army, a Socialist writer declared that the insurrection was "a turning point in the history of the working classes not only in France but in the whole world."

That writer's judgment was wrong because in fact the uprising failed to bring about change. The French government responded harshly to worker unrest, and most French employers remained indifferent to the suffering of their workers. The only reform came with the Factory Law in 1841. It echoed similar legislation in Great Britain, with such measures as prohibiting the factory employment of children under the age of eight and limiting the workday for children aged 12 to 16 to 12 hours per day. But the Factory Law applied only to establishments with more than 20 workers and to those that used steam power, so many workers remained outside the law's protection. Unlike similar British law, the French law did not appoint any inspectors to enforce its provisions.

Furthermore, unscrupulous owners easily found ways to evade the law. For example, although the Factory Law forbade children under the age of 13 from working at night, it provided an exception when a machine required repair. Owners forced the children to work at night, and if caught, simply claimed that the children were fixing broken machines. Even if caught in this lie, the owners paid only a small financial penalty.

Cartoons such as this were intended to anger workers into revolt and muster public support for factory reform. It depicts a fat bloated factory owner protected by soldiers watching down-trodden workers trudge to work in his factory.

The reforms that came in the following decades, such as the Apprentice Law of 1851, provided modest protection for workers. But the right to strike, the most powerful nonviolent way for workers to express their grievances, remained illegal. Consequently, while the French economy boomed during the years 1852 to 1857 and brought prosperity to factory owners and financiers, the working class saw little benefit.

The Franco-Prussian War (1870-1871) was a disaster for France. Following the war, France plunged into near civil war that pitted Parisians against the rest of France. Government forces lay siege to Paris, while inside the city the people experimented with a form of municipal self-government. They adopted the name "**Commune** of Paris." Brutal fighting ensued, but in the end the government overwhelmed the "Communards."

COMMUNE: in France a small district; similar to a township in the United States

The experience horrified the French middle and upper classes. They recalled that the Parisian working class had enthusiastically supported the Commune. In their determination to prevent another uprising, they supported repressive government legislation aimed at the working class. In 1872 the French government banned the International Working Men's Association (a federation of workers' groups founded by leading British and French trade union leaders that first met in London in 1864; also called the First International) and did not declare an amnesty for those who had participated in the Commune until 1880.

Nonetheless, trade unions rose again. However, the following decades witnessed the trade unions placing so much emphasis on political views that they made little actual progress in improving

The Suez Canal opened in 1869. The canal provided merchants and manufacturers in Lyons, Europe's leading silk manufacturing center, with a shorter route for transporting raw silk from the Far East.

THE INDUSTRIAL REVOLUTION AND THE WORKING CLASS

Above: When France's emperor, Napoleon III (nephew of Napoleon I), declared war on Prussia in 1870, he believed the French army was invincible. The opening battle, at Saarbrucken, gave him the first hint that this was not so.

Right: Karl Marx, one of the founders of Communism, celebrated the rebellion of the Paris Commune, describing it inaccurately as the first great uprising of the workers against their oppressors. The short reign of the Paris Commune ended (right) in brutality and bloodshed.

American workers on strike:
See also
Volume 10 pages 30–42

working conditions. In 1892 France passed a factory law that at last gave workers the same protection enjoyed in other industrialized countries. It restricted the working hours of women and children in factories and mines, but children aged 13 to 16 could still work up to 10 hours per day, while those aged 16 to 18 could work 12 hours per day. Other laws addressed worker health and the prevention of accidents. These reforms fell far short of factory laws in neighboring Germany and did not satisfy French industrial workers.

As a result, serious labor unrest continued. In 1904 alone, more than 1,000 strikes took place. Left-wing labor groups promoted what they called "direct action" against owners, by which they meant boycotts, sabotage, work slowdowns, and the obstruction of rail and postal service. Unrest grew so widespread in 1906, with over 438,000 workers involved in strikes, that many feared another revolution. Eventually the government again cracked down on radical labor leaders. In the end, as had occurred so often in French history, intense political conflict led to the neglect of troubling social issues, including the reform of working-class conditions.

GERMANY

The Industrial Revolution brought to Germany the same social problems that occurred elsewhere: long hours, low wages, severe factory discipline. As early as 1837, a reform-minded speaker addressed a provincial legislature, saying that

A craft shop in the family attic or a loom set in front of the hearth was a very different place from a large factory.

industrial capitalism had turned factory workers into slaves of their employers and of their machines. Worker unrest spread. In one typical example workers presented their complaints to a factory owner in Cologne in 1848:

"The time for hypocrisy is over and done with. When you wanted to overcome the competition of foreign rivals, you cut down our wages and you made no personal sacrifices. When you wanted to drive the goods of other German manufacturers from the home market, it was the factory hands who had to work harder for longer hours. When you aimed at artificially raising the prices of manufactured goods, you closed your works without turning a hair even though hundreds of workers were ruined."

Workers had such reasons to complain in spite of the fact that Germany had enacted more comprehensive protection for workers than other nations. For example, in 1839 the first Prussian Factory Law banned the employment of children under the age of nine. The law limited the working day for youths under the age of 16 to 10 hours while forbidding them from working at night or on Sundays and public holidays.

Early German industry:
See also
Volume 3 pages 53–56

After 1815 large numbers of Germans emigrated to the United States. Emigration acted as a safety valve by relieving the pressure of German social distress. Emigrants in their dreary quarters below decks on a trans-Atlantic vessel.

Chancellor of the Reich Otto von Bismarck believed that building strong economic links between the German states would lead to greater political unity. Napoleon III of France feared that cooperation among the German states would make Bismarck too powerful. Bismarck (right) visits his defeated rival Napoleon III (left) after Napoleon's surrender on a battlefield of the Franco-Prussian War.

Illiterate and partially literate children could only work in places where they also could attend a factory school. Furthermore, unlike similar British laws that applied only to workers in textile mills, the Prussian Factory Law applied to all factories, ironworks, and mines.

The worst cases of German poverty, unemployment, and poor living conditions did not occur among factory workers. Instead, artisans such as hand loom weavers who could not compete against factory production and small-scale farmers who could not handle the loss of common pastures and woodlots faced the worst poverty. Their distress gave rise to revolutionary movements in the 1840s. Among the publications that promoted revolution was the *Rhenish Gazette*, edited in 1842 by Karl Marx, future author of the *Communist Manifesto*.

A failed revolution in 1848 led to a decade of reaction against the working class. The government banned workers from conducting public meetings or forming trade unions. By the 1860s new worker movements emerged. When Otto von Bismarck rose to power in 1862, he devoted considerable time to economic and social issues. Bismarck recognized the growing threat of socialism. To counter that threat, he proposed novel ideas for state involvement, such as compulsory worker insurance against accidents, sickness, and old age. For example, the Accident Insurance Law of 1884 compelled employers to pay the entire cost of insuring some 13 million workers against workplace accidents. If a worker died from an accident (about 15 industrial accidents in 100 were fatal at that time), his widow received a burial payment, weekly pension, and allowance for each dependent child.

These programs were far ahead of anything anywhere else. They provided German workers with a real sense of security: Workers benefitted from improved work conditions, housing, sanitation, and medical care. Eventually, the world's other advanced industrial nations adopted welfare programs similar to those Germany put in place between 1884 and 1889.

In Germany these programs failed to meet one of Bismarck's goals—preventing German workers from joining socialist organizations and political parties. By 1910 about 80 percent of all workers who belonged to labor organizations were in socialist unions. However, the workers' revolution that Communist leaders predicted would occur in Germany failed to take place. Instead, revolution came to Russia.

RUSSIA

In 1844 the Russian government investigated the cause of

Russian child labor laws proved difficult to enforce. People lied about the ages of child employees, and the few inspectors could not begin to cover such a vast area as Russia. Russian boys employed by a woodworking shop in 1884.

recent worker unrest outside of Moscow. Inspectors found that the region's 23 cotton-spinning mills employed over 2,000 children, and that the children worked on both day and night shifts. The czar (emperor) issued an edict prohibiting night shifts for children under 12, but owners paid no attention. More important to them was the 1845 law that banned industrial strikes. In the absence of strikes the owners could continue to exploit workers however they wanted.

In 1867 Karl Marx wrote that in Russia "the horrors of the early days of the British factory system are still in full bloom." During the next decade conditions did not improve. Twelve and fourteen hour workdays for factory laborers were common. Wages were low, and workers faced arbitrary fines. Working conditions were unhealthy and often dangerous. Workers lived like herded animals in factory barracks provided by the employer.

Early Russian industrialization:
See also
Volume 6 pages 46–61

Housing for Russian factory workers.

Czar Alexander II ruled Russia from 1855 until his assassination in 1881, a period coinciding with much of the nation's industrial expansion. Alexander II emancipated the serfs in 1861, modernized many aspects of Russia's government, and expanded Russia's Asian territory. A group of terrorists aiming to overthrow the government made several attempts on his life before they succeeded in killing him with a bomb.

These woeful conditions led to two movements of great historical significance. In the 1870s a group of middle-class intellectuals formed a socialist organization. They believed that the czar's backing of industrial capitalism had caused the nation great distress. Their efforts to spread their beliefs brought them harsh exile in Siberia. Some of the survivors formed a secret society, members of whom assassinated Czar Alexander II in 1881.

Also in the 1870s industrial workers formed various union-like organizations. The police squashed them, but some students rallied to their cause. Worker and student demonstrations and factory strikes followed. At one memorable trial a socialist leader predicted that some time in the near future millions of workers would rise to overthrow the ruling class.

As labor unrest spread, in 1882 a government edict finally addressed factory working conditions. But even simple regulations like prohibiting child labor in factories proved difficult to enforce. Furthermore, while such measures as the Factory Law of 1886 increased worker protection, the prohibition against unions continued, and penalties for strikes increased. And so the pattern continued—workers demanding factory reform, the government responding with partial

A Russian woodworking shop equipped with machinery imported from Germany.

Russia's communist revolution:
See also
Volume 6 pages 62–63

reform, and most industrialists ignoring the law without consequence.

Then a new labor organization, the Russian Social Democratic Workers Party, launched a revolutionary movement. Led by Vladimir Lenin, the party's aim was to end the power of the landed gentry and the factory-owning capitalists, and substitute a socialist republic. The ensuing conflict proved long, complex, and bloody, but in the end the Union of Soviet Socialist Republics arose with Lenin at its helm.

CONCLUSION

In industrialized nations social reformers and members of the working class saw the wealth and power of the ruling class, capitalists, and business owners. They contrasted what they observed with the long hours of drudgery and stark poverty of the men, women, and children of the working class. The majority of the workers on whom national prosperity depended reaped little reward for their labor. Those who possessed wealth and power would give up nothing without a fight. Inevitably, workers and those who shared their goals joined forces to achieve better working and living conditions by whatever means they could. Although some nations overcame strikes and civil disturbances to change their social structures through legal and orderly means, others could not bring about change without violent revolution.

Disagreements caused the Russian Social Democratic Workers Party to split into factions. During World War I Lenin believed that his party should take advantage of the opportunity to overthrow the Russian government. Other party members instead felt that it was their patriotic duty to fight for Russia and win the war. Lenin and his supporters in a secret meeting.

A DATELINE OF MAJOR EVENTS DURING THE INDUSTRIAL REVOLUTION

	BEFORE 1750	1760	1770	1780
REVOLUTIONS IN INDUSTRY AND TECHNOLOGY	**1619:** English settlers establish the first iron works in colonial America, near Jamestown, Virginia. **1689:** Thomas Savery (England) patents the first design for a steam engine. **1709:** Englishman Abraham Darby uses coke instead of coal to fuel his blast furnace. **1712:** Englishman Thomas Newcomen builds the first working steam engine. **1717:** Thomas Lombe establishes a silk-throwing factory in England. **1720:** The first Newcomen steam engine on the Continent is installed at a Belgian coal mine. **1733:** James Kay (England) invents the flying shuttle. **1742:** Benjamin Huntsman begins making crucible steel in England.	**1756:** The first American coal mine opens. **1764:** In England James Hargreaves invents the spinning jenny. **1769:** Englishman Richard Arkwright patents his spinning machine, called a water frame. James Watt of Scotland patents an improved steam engine design. Josiah Wedgwood (England) opens his Etruria pottery works.	**1771:** An industrial spy smuggles drawings of the spinning jenny from England to France. **1774:** John Wilkinson (England) builds machines for boring cannon cylinders. **1775:** Arkwright patents carding, drawing, and roving machines. In an attempt to end dependence on British textiles American revolutionaries open a spinning mill in Philadelphia using a smuggled spinning-jenny design. **1777:** Oliver Evans (U.S.) invents a card-making machine. **1778:** John Smeaton (England) introduces cast iron gearing to transfer power from waterwheels to machinery. The water closet (indoor toilet) is invented in England. **1779:** Englishman Samuel Crompton develops the spinning mule.	**1783:** Englishman Thomas Bell invents a copper cylinder to print patterns on fabrics. **1784:** Englishman Henry Cort invents improved rollers for rolling mills and the puddling process for refining pig iron. Frenchman Claude Berthollet discovers that chlorine can be used as a bleach. The ironworks at Le Creusot use France's first rotary steam engine to power its hammers, as well as using the Continent's first coke-fired blast furnace. **1785:** Englishman Edmund Cartwright invents the power loom. **1788:** The first steam engine is imported into Germany.
REVOLUTIONS IN TRANSPORTATION AND COMMUNICATION		**1757:** The first canal is built in England.  Locks on an English canal		**1785:** The first canal is built in the United States, at Richmond, Virginia. **1787:** John Fitch and James Rumsey (U.S.) each succeed in launching a working steamboat.
SOCIAL REVOLUTIONS	**1723:** Britain passes an act to allow the establishment of workhouses for the poor.	**1750:** The enclosure of common land gains momentum in Britain.	**1776:** Scottish professor Adam Smith publishes *The Wealth of Nations*, which promotes laissez-faire capitalism.	 The workhouse
INTERNATIONAL RELATIONS	 Continental Army in winter quarters at Valley Forge		**1775–1783:** The American Revolution. Thirteen colonies win their independence from Great Britain and form a new nation, the United States of America.	**1789–1793:** The French Revolution leads to abolition of the monarchy and execution of the king and queen. Mass executions follow during the Reign of Terror, 1793–1794.

1790	1800	1810	1820

1790: English textile producer Samuel Slater begins setting up America's first successful textile factory in Pawtucket, Rhode Island.

Jacob Perkins (U.S.) invents a machine capable of mass-producing nails.

1791: French chemist Nicholas Leblanc invents a soda-making process.

1793: Eli Whitney (U.S.) invents a cotton gin.

1794: Germany's first coke-fired blast furnace is built.

The first German cotton spinning mill installs Arkwright's water frame.

1798: Eli Whitney devises a system for using power-driven machinery to produce interchangeable parts, the model for the "American System" of manufacture.

Wool-spinning mills are built in Belgium using machinery smuggled out of England.

A cylindrical papermaking machine is invented in England.

1801: American inventor Oliver Evans builds the first working high-pressure steam engine and uses it to power a mill.

Joseph-Marie Jacquard (France) invents a loom that uses punch cards to produce patterned fabrics.

A cotton-spinning factory based on British machinery opens in Belgium.

The first cotton-spinning mill in Switzerland begins operation.

Austria establishes the Continent's largest cotton-spinning mill.

1802: In England William Murdock uses coal gas to light an entire factory.

Richard Trevithick builds a high-pressure steam engine in England.

1807: British businessmen open an industrial complex in Belgium that includes machine manufacture, coal mining, and iron production.

1808: Russia's first spinning mill begins production in Moscow.

1810: Henry Maudslay (England) invents the precision lathe.

1816: Steam power is used for the first time in an American paper mill.

English scientist Humphry Davy invents a safety lamp for coal miners in England.

1817: The French iron industry's first puddling works and rolling mills are established.

1819: Thomas Blanchard (U.S.) invents a gunstock-turning lathe, which permits production of standardized parts.

A turning lathe

1821: Massachusetts businessmen begin developing Lowell as a site for textile mills.

1822: Power looms are introduced in French factories.

1820s: Spinning mills begin operation in Sweden.

Steam power is first used in Czech industry.

1827: A water-driven turbine is invented in France.

1794: The 66-mile Philadelphia and Lancaster turnpike begins operation.

Along an American Highway

1802: In England Richard Trevithick builds his first steam locomotive.

1807: Robert Fulton launches the Clermont, the first commercially successful steamboat, on the Hudson River in New York.

1811: Robert Fulton and his partner launch the first steamboat on the Mississippi River.

Construction begins on the Cumberland Road (later renamed the National Road) from Baltimore, Maryland, to Wheeling, Virginia.

1815: In England John McAdam develops an improved technique for surfacing roads.

1819: The first steamship crosses the Atlantic Ocean.

1825: The 363-mile Erie Canal is completed in America.

In England the first passenger railroad, the Stockton and Darlington Railway, begins operation.

1826: The 2-mile horse-drawn Granite Railroad in Massachusetts becomes the first American railroad.

1790: First American patent law passed.

Philadelphia begins building a public water system.

1798: Robert Owen takes over the New Lanark mills and begins implementing his progressive ideas.

1800: Parliament prohibits most labor union activity.

1802: Parliament passes a law limiting the working hours of poor children and orphans.

1811–1816: Luddite rioters destroy textile machinery in England.

1819: Parliament extends legal protection to all child laborers.

British cavalry fire at demonstrators demanding voting reform in Manchester, killing 11 and wounding hundreds, including women and children.

1827: Carpenters organize the first national trade union in Britain.

1799: Napoleon Bonaparte seizes control of France's government.

1792–1815: The Napoleonic Wars involve most of Europe, Great Britain, and Russia. France occupies many of its neighboring nations, reorganizes their governments, and changes their borders.

1812–1815: War between the United States and Great Britain disrupts America's foreign trade and spurs the development of American industry.

18th-century carpenter

A DATELINE OF MAJOR EVENTS DURING THE INDUSTRIAL REVOLUTION

	1830	1840	1850	1860
REVOLUTIONS IN INDUSTRY AND TECHNOLOGY	1830: Switzerland's first weaving mill established. 1831: British researcher Michael Faraday builds an electric generator. American inventor Cyrus McCormick builds a horse-drawn mechanical reaper. 1834: Bulgaria's first textile factory is built. 1835: Samuel Colt (U.S)invents the Colt revolver. The first steam engine is used to power a paper mill in Croatia. 1836: The first Hungarian steam mill, the Pest Rolling Mill company, begins using steam power to process grain. 1837: The first successful coke-fired blast furnace in the United States begins operation.	American blacksmith John Deere introduces the first steel plow. 1842: Britain lifts restrictions on exporting textile machinery. Making Bessemer steel	1849: The California Gold Rush begins. 1850: Swedish sawmills begin using steam power. 1851: The Great Exhibition opens at the Crystal Palace in London. William Kelly of Kentucky invents a process for converting pig iron to steel. 1852: Hydraulic mining is introduced in the American West. 1853: The first cotton-spinning mill opens in India. 1856: William Perkin (England) synthesizes the first coal tar dye. Henry Bessemer (England) announces his process for converting pig iron to steel. Isaac Singer (U.S.) introduces the sewing machine.	1859: Edwin Drake successfully drills for oil in Pennsylvania. 1863: Ernest Solvay of Belgium begins working on a process to recover ammonia from soda ash in order to produce bleaching powder. 1864: Switzerland's first major chemical company is established. The Siemens-Martin open-hearth steelmaking process is perfected in France. 1865: The first oil pipeline opens in America. The rotary web press is invented in America, permitting printing on both sides of the paper. 1866: U.S. government surveyors discover the largest-known deposit of iron ore in the world in the Mesabi Range of northern Minnesota.
REVOLUTIONS IN TRANSPORTATION AND COMMUNICATION	1830: The first locomotive-powered railroad to offer regular service begins operating in South Carolina. The opening of the Liverpool and Manchester Railway marks the beginning of the British railroad boom. 1833: The 60-mile Camden and Amboy Railroad of New Jersey is completed. 1835: Construction begins on Germany's first railroad.	1836: First railroad built in Russia. 1843: Tunnel completed under the Thames River, London, England, the world's first to be bored through soft clay under a riverbed. 1844: Samuel Morse (U.S.) sends the first message via his invention, the telegraph. The nation's first steam-powered sawmill begins operation on the West Coast.	1846: First railroad built in Hungary. 1853: The first railway is completed in India. 1854: Americans complete the Moscow-St. Petersburg railroad line. 1855: Switzerland's first railroad opens.	1859: In France Etienne Lenoir invents an internal combustion engine. 1860–1861: The Pony Express, a system of relay riders, carries mail to and from America's West Coast. 1866: The transatlantic telegraph cable is completed. Congress authorizes construction of a transcontinental telegraph line. 1869: The tracks of two railroad companies meet at Promontory, Utah, to complete America's first transcontinental railroad
SOCIAL REVOLUTIONS	1833: Parliament passes the Factory Act to protect children working in textile factories. 1836–1842: The English Chartist movement demands Parliamentary reform, but its petitions are rejected by Parliament. 1838: The U.S. Congress passes a law regulating steamboat boiler safety, the first attempt by the federal government to regulate private behavior in the interest of public safety.	1842: Parliament bans the employment of children and women underground in mines. 1845: Russia bans strikes. 1847: A new British Factory Act limits working hours to 10 hours a day or 58 hours a week for children aged 13 to 18 and for women. 1848: Marx and Engels coauthor the Communist Manifesto.	1854: In England Charles Dickens publishes *Hard Times*, a novel based on his childhood as a factory worker. 1857: Brooklyn, New York, builds a city wastewater system.	1860–1910: More than 20 million Europeans emigrate to the United States. 1866: National Labor Union forms in the United States. 1869: Knights of Labor forms in the United States. Founding of the Great Atlantic and Pacific Tea Company (A&P) in the U.S.
INTERNATIONAL RELATIONS	1839–1842: Great Britain defeats China in a war and forces it to open several ports to trade.	1847: Austro-Hungary occupies Italy. 1848: Failed revolutions take place in France, Germany, and Austro-Hungary. Serfdom ends in Austro-Hungary.	1853: The American naval officer Commodore Matthew Perry arrives in Japan. 1853–1856: France, Britain, and Turkey defeat Russia in the Crimean War. 1858: Great Britain takes control of India, retaining it until 1947.	1861–1865: The American Civil War brings about the end of slavery in the United States and disrupts raw cotton supplies for U.S. and foreign cotton mills. 1867: Britain gains control of parts of Malaysia. Malaysia is a British colony from 1890 to 1957.

1870	1880	1890	1900

1860s: Agricultural machinery introduced in Hungary.

1870: John D. Rockefeller establishes the Standard Oil Company (U.S.).

1873: The Bethlehem Steel Company begins operation in Pennsylvania.

1875: The first modern iron and steel works opens in India.

Investment in the Japan's cotton industry booms.

1876: Philadelphia hosts the Centennial Exposition.

1877: Hungary installs its first electrical system.

1879: Charles Brush builds the nation's first arc-lighting system in San Francisco.

Thomas Edison (U.S.) develops the first practical incandescent light bulb.

1870s: Japan introduces mechanical silk-reeling.

1882: In New York City the Edison Electric Illuminating Company begins operating the world's first centralized electrical generating station.

1884: The U.S. Circuit Court bans hydraulic mining.

George Westinghouse (U.S.) founds Westinghouse Electric Company.

English engineer Charles Parsons develops a steam turbine.

1885: The introduction of band saws makes American lumbering more efficient.

German inventor Carl Benz builds a self-propelled vehicle powered by a single cylinder gas engine with electric ignition.

1887: An English power plant is the first to use steam turbines to generate electricity.

1888: Nikola Tesla (U.S.) invents an

alternating current electric motor.

1894: An American cotton mill becomes the first factory ever built to rely entirely on electric power.

1895: George Westinghouse builds the world's first generating plant designed to transmit power over longer distances—a hydroelectric plant at Niagara Falls to

transmit alternating current some 20 miles to consumers in Buffalo, New York.

1901: The United States Steel Corporation is formed by a merger of several American companies.

Japan opens its first major iron and steel works.

1929: The U.S.S.R. begins implementing its first Five-Year Plan, which places nationwide industrial development under central government control.

Power generators at Edison Electric

1875: Japan builds its first railway.

1876: In the U.S. Alexander Graham Bell invents the telephone.

German inventor Nikolaus Otto produces a practical gasoline engine.

1870s: Sweden's railroad boom.

1883: Brooklyn Bridge completed.

1885: Germans Gottlieb Daimler and Wilhelm Maybach build the world's first motorcycle.

1886: Daimler and Maybach invent the carburetor, the device that efficiently mixes fuel and air in internal combustion engines

1888: The first electric urban streetcar system begins operation in Richmond, Virginia.

1893: American brothers Charles and J. Frank Duryea build a working gasoline-powered automobile.

1896: Henry Ford builds a demonstration car powered by an internal combustion engine.

1896–1904: Russia builds the Manchurian railway in China.

1903: Henry Ford establishes Ford Motor Company.

1904: New York City subway system opens.

Trans-Siberian Railroad completed.

1908: William Durant, maker of horse-drawn carriages, forms the General Motors Company.

1909: Ford introduces the Model T automobile.

1870: Parliament passes a law to provide free schooling for poor children.

1872: France bans the International Working Men's Association.

1874: France applies its child labor laws to all industrial establishments and provides for inspectors to enforce the laws.

1877: Wage cuts set off the Great Railroad Strike in West Virginia, and the strike spreads across the country. Federal troops kill 35 strikers.

1880: Parliament makes school attendance compulsory for children between the ages of 5 and 10.

1881: India passes a factory law limiting child employment.

1884: Germany passes a law requiring employers to provide insurance against workplace accidents.

1886: American Federation of Labor forms.

1887: U.S. Interstate Commerce Act passed to regulate railroad freight charges.

1890: The U.S. government outlaws monopolies with passage of the Sherman Antitrust Act.

1892: Workers strike at Carnegie Steel in Homestead, Pennsylvania, in response to wage cuts. An armed confrontation results in 12 deaths.

1894: The Pullman strike, called in response to wage cuts, halts American railroad traffic. A confrontation with 2,000 federal troops kills 12 strikers in Chicago.

1900: Japan passes a law to limit union activity.

1902: The United Mine Workers calls a nationwide strike against coal mines, demanding eight-hour workdays and higher wages.

1903: Socialists organize the Russian Social Democratic Workers Party.

1931: Japan passes a law to limit working hours for women and children in textile factories.

1870: The city-states of Italy unify to form one nation.

1871: Parisians declare self-government in the city but are defeated by government forces.

Prussia and the other German states unify to form the German Empire.

1877–1878: War between Russia and Turkey. Bulgaria gains independence from Turkey.

1900–1901: A popular uprising supported by the Chinese government seeks to eject all foreigners from China.

1917: Russian Revolution

1929: A worldwide economic depression begins.

REVOLUTIONARY THINKERS

FRIEDRICH ENGELS: 1820–1895; born in Germany. The son of an industrialist who owned cotton mills in Germany and England, Engels joined the family business. In addition to his business pursuits he wrote poetry, sang in a chorus, and enjoyed athletic pursuits. He spent a year serving in an artillery regiment and met Karl Marx at a university lecture. In 1842 Engels moved to Manchester, England, and resumed working for the family business; it was there that he observed the gap between the working class and the wealthy. He traveled to Europe and collaborated with Marx to promote communism, and together they tried to influence the course of the 1848 revolution to bring about communism in Germany. The revolution failed, and both Engels and Marx ended up living in England. Engels continued to work for the family business while writing articles promoting communism and supporting Marx with a portion of his earnings. (See pages 33–35 of this volume for more about Engels.)

VLADIMIR LENIN: 1870–1924; born Vladimir Ilich Ulyanov in Russia. Part of a closely knit and well-educated middle-class family, young Vladimir may have been driven to embrace revolution when his older brother was executed for plotting to assassinate the czar. The Russian government then treated the entire Ulyanov family as criminal suspects. Overcoming official obstacles, Vladimir earned a degree in law and became an expert in the communist theories of Karl Marx. In 1895 the government sentenced him to exile in Siberia for organizing Marxist groups and promoting Marxism among Russian workers. His fiancee, also a Marxist, joined him in exile, and the two married in Siberia. On regaining his freedom in 1900, Vladimir Ulyanov changed his last name to Lenin and continued his communist activities in western Europe. After the czarist government fell in 1917, Lenin returned to Russia to lead the revolutionary government. He redistributed land and wealth, survived an assassin's bullets, kept his party in power through a civil war, ruthlessly suppressed opposition, and remained the head of state until his death. During the years of illness leading to his death, Lenin engaged in a losing power struggle with Joseph Stalin, whom he saw betraying socialist ideals for the sake of totalitarian power.

WILLIAM LOVETT: 1800–1877; born in England. Lovett was a cabinetmaker who taught himself economics and politics. He supported the utopian ideas of Robert Owen and helped found an early workers' association. After leading the Chartist movement, campaigning unsuccessfully to reform Parliament, and spending a year in prison for his political activities, Lovett worked as a teacher and wrote textbooks for working-class children.

KARL MARX: 1818–1883; born in Germany. Marx studied history and philosophy, received a doctoral degree, and became a newspaper editor. When his newspaper was shut down for its views in 1843, Marx left Germany and moved to Paris with his wife. Around the time Marx published the famous *Communist Manifesto* in 1848, revolution broke out in France and Germany, allowing him to return to Germany and restart his newspaper. He used his newspaper to influence the revolutionaries in favor of communism, but the revolution failed. Marx was expelled from Germany and settled in England. Supported by Friedrich Engels, Marx spent long hours in the library of the British Museum formulating his ideas about capitalism and the working class. The first volume of *Das Kapital* appeared in 1867. Marx hoped to replace capitalism with socialism throughout the world.

ROBERT OWEN: 1771–1858; born in Wales. Owen went to work at the age of 10 and at 18 borrowed money to start his own business producing machinery for textile mills. He later became the owner of the New Lanark cotton mill, where he provided decent housing and a school for his workers, and promoted trade unions. As a social reformer dedicated to socialist utopian ideals, Owen tried to establish cooperative profit-sharing communities, including one at New Harmony, Indiana, in America, but the communities failed. (See pages 12–13 of this volume for more about Owen.)

JOSEPH PAXTON: 1801–1868; born in England. Paxton started out as a gardener for an English duke and advanced to designing the gardens and greenhouses on his employer's estate. Paxton based his design for the Crystal Palace on one of his greenhouses. Two thousand workers erected it in less than six months. Paxton also served in Parliament, managed a railway, and designed houses and public parks.

ROBERT PEEL: 1750–1830; born in England. The son of a calico printer, Peel ran the family business and expanded it to encompass 23 mills with 15,000 employees. As a member of Parliament he campaigned for laws to protect child laborers. Peel's son also served in Parliament and eventually became the prime minister of Great Britain.

ADAM SMITH: 1723–1790; born in Scotland. Among his many academic achievements Smith set forth in his writings persuasive arguments in favor of unrestricted capitalism. In addition to writing and lecturing about economics, Smith's career included positions as a university professor, private tutor, and government official. (See pages 31–33 of this volume for more about Smith.)

GLOSSARY

AMNESTY: a general pardon issued by a government

ARTISANS: skilled craftsmen who worked in such trades as shoemaking, printing, or making cutlery

BOYCOTT: an agreement to refuse to buy from or sell to certain businesses

CAPITAL: money or property used in operating a business

CAPITALISM: the economic system in which property and businesses are privately owned and operated for personal profit

CAPITALIST: a person who invests money in a business

CHARTER: a document setting out the rules for operating an organization

CHARTIST: supporter of an English political movement that tried and failed to reform Parliament and make it more responsive to the people

COLLECTIVE: acting together for a common cause

COMMUNE: in France a small district; similar to a township in the United States

COMMUNISM: a political system in which the community or government owns all property and operates all businesses with the aim of sharing the work and profits equally; as practiced by the Communist Party, it resulted in brutal suppression of all opposition.

COTTAGE INDUSTRY: manufacturing goods at home

CUTLER: artisan who makes or repairs metal cutting tools, such as knives

GUILD: medieval form of trade association, whereby skilled workers in the same craft or trade organized to protect their business interests

LAISSEZ-FAIRE: French for let [people] do [what they please]; refers to an economic system in which businesses can operate without any government regulation

OPERATIVE: one who operates a machine in a factory

PARLIAMENT: the legislature of Great Britain, consisting of an upper house called the House of Lords and a lower house called the House of Commons

PENCE: plural of penny, a unit of British money

PIECER: spinning mill worker, usually a child, who tied together the ends of broken threads; sometimes called a "piecener"

SHILLING: a unit of British money, a silver coin equal to a certain number of pence

SOCIALISM: an economic system in which the community owns all property and operates all businesses with the aim of sharing the work and profits equally; Communists viewed socialism as an intermediate stage in the evolution from capitalism to communism.

STOCKINGER: one who knits stockings

SUFFRAGE: the right to vote

SWEATED TRADES: trades in which workers endure long hours, low pay, and poor working conditions

SWEATSHOP: a workplace where workers are forced to endure long hours, low pay, and poor conditions

TRADE UNION: association of workers for the purpose of obtaining better wages and working conditions

TRANSPORTATION: forced removal from Great Britain to one of its colonies, a sentence inflicted on people convicted of breaking the law

UTOPIA: imaginary island with a perfect political and social system, from a book with that name written in 1516 by Sir Thomas More

UTOPIAN: an idealist who tries to design and establish a perfect community

VICTORIAN: typical of the time when Queen Victoria ruled Great Britain (1837-1901)

WARPING: spinning thread suitable for use as warp threads in weaving. The warp is the strong thread that runs the length of woven cloth.

WORKHOUSE: in England a place of confinement and forced labor for unemployed poor people

ADDITIONAL RESOURCES

BOOKS:

Bland, Celia. *The Mechanical Age: The Industrial Revolution in England*. New York: Facts on File, 1995.

Dickens, Charles. *David Copperfield*.

Dickens, Charles. *Hard Times*.

Dickens, Charles. *Oliver Twist*.

Lines, Clifford. *Companion to the Industrial Revolution*. New York: Facts on File, 1990

Mitchell, Sally. *Daily Life in Victorian England*. Westport, CT: Greenwood Press, 1996.

Moynahan, Brian. *The Russian Century: A Photographic History of Russia's Hundred Years*. New York: Random House, 1994.

WEBSITES:

http://www.alexanderpalace.org/mainpage.html
Alexander Palace Time Machine: images and essays about one of the czars who ruled Russia during its industrial revolution.

http://www.bbc.co.uk/history/lj/victorian_britainlj/preview.shtml
Links to articles and games about industry and society in Victorian England

http://www.dke-encyc.com
Search using "industrial revolution" for links to articles about the Industrial Revolution in Victorian England

http://www.fordham.edu/halsall/mod/modsbook14.html
Internet Modern History Sourcebook: Industrial Revolution—provides links to excerpts from historical texts

http://www.library.nwu.edu/spec/siege.index.html
Images of the 1870 siege of the Paris Commune.

http://www.spartacus.schoolnet.co.uk/IRchild.htm
Child labor in England 1750-1850

SET INDEX

Bold numbers refer to volumes

A

B

C

R

railroads
  Belgium **3**:42
  China **7**:28
  Eastern Europe **6**:32–34
  Germany **3**:54–55
  Great Britain **3**:15, 26–30, 61
  India **7**:30–31
  Japan **7**:18–20
  locomotives **3**:26–29; **5**:31–35, 40–41; **6**:27, 54–55
  Russia **6**:53–56
  U.S. **5**:17–18, 28–41, 50, 57; **8**:4–7, 27–29, 52, 55; **10**:26, 40–41, 58–59
Radcliffe, William **2**:15
Revolution, American **4**:20–23, 33, 41, 44; **5**:59
Revolution, French **3**:38–40, 42, 44–45
Revolution of 1848 **6**:33; **9**:14, 55
Revolution, Russian **6**:61–63; **9**:61
Rhode Island **4**:27, 34–35, 40
roads **3**:16–22; **5**:8–11, 29; **8**:36
robber barons **8**:31; **10**:33, 36
Rockefeller, John D. **8**:29–31, 66; **10**:47, 56, 60
Roebuck, John **2**:32, 34, 41–42, 65
Rogers, Moses **3**:32
rolling mills **2**:36; **4**:52, 54–55, 61
Romania **6**:42–43, 63
Roosevelt, Theodore **10**:31
roving (textile) **4**:22
Royal Society **3**:58–60
Rumsey, James **5**:20, 67
Rush, Benjamin **4**:17
Russia **6**:38–41, 46–63; **9**:57–61; **10**:5
  agriculture **6**:50, 52
  coal **6**:55
  communism **6**:62–63
  foreign investment **6**:53, 56, 58, 60
  government **6**:57-58, 60–61
  iron and steel industry **6**:49, 55–56
  oil **6**:59
  population **6**:51, 57
  poverty **6**:48, 52
  railroads **6**:53–55

  revolution **6**:62–63; **9**:61
  social inequality **6**:48, 51
  textile industry **6**:48–49, 51, 57; **9**:58
  working conditions **9**:58–60

S

St. Louis, Missouri **5**:25–27; **10**:45
St. Petersburg, Russia **6**:53, 58
salt **1**:43
San Francisco, California **10**:48
Savery, Thomas **2**:27–28, 65
sawmills **6**:16–17, 29; **8**:8–9
Scotland **1**:24, 46, 48; **2**:26, 42–43; **3**:19, 31, 53; **7**:31; **9**:12–13, 31, 40
Sellers, Nathan **4**:61
Serbia **6**:44
serfs **6**:33–34, 51–52; **9**:59
sewing machines **8**:24–25
Shanghai, China **7**:25–26
Sheffield, England **2**:37–40
shipbuilding **1**:39; **3**:9; **6**:8, 22; **7**:16, 56
shuttle, flying **2**:10, 20–22
Siemens, Frederick **7**:53, 67
Siemens, William **7**:53, 67
silk **1**:35; **6**:23–26, 41; **7**:11–13, 15, 22; **9**:51
Singapore **7**:35
Singer, Isaac **8**:24–25, 66
Slater Mill **4**:24–27
Slater, Samuel **4**:23, 26–27, 29, 49
slavery **4**:44–45, 58–60; **9**:25; **10**:24–25
Sliven, Bulgaria **6**:40
Smeaton, John **2**:35, 66; **3**:48, 67
Smith, Adam **9**:31–33, 67
smuggling **3**:42, 44–45; **4**:23, 32
social class **1**:25–30; **3**:34; **4**:4, 58; **6**:28, 30, 33, 48, 51–52, 62; **7**:30, 44; **8**:23; **9**:8–9, 35, 37, 42–43, 51, 61; **10**:5, 8, 10, 56
social reformers
  Chartist movement **9**:11, 14–15
  Debs, Eugene **10**:40, 42–43, 67

automobiles **8**:33–40

canals **3**:22–25, 34, 43; **5**:12–15, 18, 50; **9**:50–51; **10**:4–5

horse–drawn wagons **3**:16–20, 26–28; **5**:4–5, 8, 10, 28–30, 50; **7**:27, 30; **8**:5, 27

railroads **3**:15, 26–30, 42, 54–55, 61; **5**:17–18, 28–41, 50, 57; **6**:32–34, 53–56; **7**:18–20, 28, 30–31; **8**:4–7, 27–29, 52, 55; **10**:26, 40–41, 58–59

roads **3**:16–22; **5**:8–11, 29; **8**:36

steamboats **3**:30–33; **5**:17, 19–27, 50

urban **8**:50–51 **10**:52–54

Trevithick, Richard **3**:15, 26–28, 67; **5**:22

trusts **8**:30–31; **10**:56

turbines **3**:49; **5**:45; **6**:51; **7**:48–49

Turin, Italy **6**:26

Turkey **6**:37, 38, 40–41

U

unions **7**:21; **8**:15; **9**:10–12, 15, 51, 57, 60; **10**:5, 23, 28–31, 36, 38, 40, 42

American Federation of Labor **10**:30–31

American Railway Union **10**:40, 42

Knights of Labor **10**:28–30, 38

National Labor Union **10**:28

United Mine Workers **10**:38

United States

agriculture **4**:7–8, 58–59; **5**:39, 48; **8**:16–23, 59; **10**:18, 45, 56

child labor **4**:11, 13, 28; **8**:21; **10**:11, 14–16, 18–23

colonial period **4**:4–21

corporations **5**:57–61; **8**:31–32, 38–40, 42, 47–48, 51, 54; **10**:36, 39–42 56, 60–61

cottage industry **4**:7, 10–13; **10**:4, 18

environment **8**:9–12; **9**:37–38, 41;

10:48, 51–52, 60

factories **4**:24–27, 42–43, 46–48, 52; **5**:40, 44–47, 50; **7**:52, 61; **8**:55; **10**:6–8, 12, 17, 27, 34–35, 46–47

factory towns **4**:27–28, 34–35; **5**:42–54; **10**:39, 45

government and law **5**:16–17, 24; **8**:12, 31; **10**:20, 34, 36, 40, 56, 58–60

housing **5**:48–49; **10**:9–10, 56–59

immigrants **4**:5, 29, 59; **5**:48, 54; **6**:17–19; **8**:24, 64–66; **10**:10–11, 15–16, 23, 45

industrial accidents **5**:24, 35–37; **7**:58; **8**:14–15; **10**:12–13, 15–16, 19

iron and steel industry **4**:14–17, 23, 52–55, 61; **5**:39; **8**:52–53, 55, 58–59; **10**:24, 26, 60

mining **8**:10–15; **10**:18–19, 22–23

oil industry **8**:4, 26–31; **10**:56

population **4**:5, 16, 60; **5**:4–7; **8**:11; **10**:45

poverty **4**:4, 58; **8**:22–23; **10**:5, 8, 10, 56

strikes and protests **5**:48; **8**:54; **10**:5, 24–25, 29–31, 34–42

textile industry **4**:11–13, 19, 22–29, 40, 44–45, 49, 58–59; **5**:42–54, 53–54; **10**:6–8, 17, 27, 46–47

transportation **5**:4–5, 8–15, 17–41, 50, 57; **8**:4–7, 27–29, 33–40, 50–52, 55; **10**:4–5, 26, 40–41, 52–54, 58–59

unions **8**:15; **10**:5, 23, 28–31, 36, 38, 40, 42

women **4**:11, 28; **5**:48–49; **10**:11

Ure, Andrew **9**:20–21, 46

V

Van Buren, Martin **5**:24

Venice, Italy **6**:22–23

Verviers, Belgium **3**:40

Victoria (queen of Great Britain) **9**:8, 41